Wild in the Dawn

poems by

Rob Hunter

Finishing Line Press
Georgetown, Kentucky

Wild
in the Dawn

Copyright © 2023 by Rob Hunter
ISBN 979-8-88838-098-7 First Edition
All rights reserved under International and Pan-American Copyright Conventions. No part of this book may be reproduced in any manner whatsoever without written permission from the publisher, except in the case of brief quotations embodied in critical articles and reviews.

ACKNOWLEDGMENTS

Some of the poems in this collection were first published in the following:

The Dementia Patients, *Poet Lore*
Drowning in Vermont, *The Oddville Press*
Secret. Lovers, The Same Rain, *Sleet*
Pet, *Wild Violet*
Invisible Shells, *Straight Forward Poetry*
For a Taste of Honey, *Timberline Review*
Transfer Station, *Foliate Oak*
Alarm, Instead, The Silver Bowl, *Rat's Ass Review*
Fire, *Gray Sparrow Review*
School Teacher, *Sheila-Na-Gig Online*
You were a Blue Lake, *Oakwood*

Publisher: Leah Huete de Maines
Editor: Christen Kincaid
Cover Art: Susanne Nilsson, *Dawn*, (CC BY-SA 2.0), https://flickr.com/photos/55856449@N04/32701232024
Author Photo: Rob Hunter
Cover Design: Elizabeth Maines McCleavy

Order online: www.finishinglinepress.com
also available on amazon.com

Author inquiries and mail orders:
Finishing Line Press
PO Box 1626
Georgetown, Kentucky 40324
USA

Table of Contents

Instead 1

Vermont Neighbors 2

Pet 3

Fire 5

Invisible Shells 6

School Teacher 7

The Same Rain 8

For a Taste of Honey 9

The Dementia Patients 10

Jealousy Coat 11

The Poison Tree 12

Baptism 13

Secret. Lovers. 14

Alarm 15

Drowning in Vermont 16

Recovery 18

Transfer Station Scene 19

After Mowing 20

For the Sparrows in the Newark Liberty International Airport ... 21

Public Pool 22

Wild in the Dawn 23

Late August 24

You were a Blue Lake 25

The Silver Bowl 26

for Sarah and Stevie

Instead

Some summer mornings
instead of the musical kaleidoscope
of the songbirds
feathering my yard's trees
and hanging feeders

I'll wake to several crows
yelling obscenities
at each other out on the lawn,
a pack of miscreants
who've been out all-night drinking:
their arguing
a chainsaw in the dawn.

But right now
a single crow
flaps its big wings once, twice,
slips sideways in flight
through a hail of slanting snow,
the daring first stroke
of black on a fresh
white canvas.

Vermont Neighbors

The neighbors drive up about six times a year. They have our number and we theirs. If something needs checking, like the heat. They heard we were having a hard freeze last October, called to ask if I could check, see if the thermostat is right, the hot air billowing out of the grate on the first floor floor. A few winters ago their pipes froze, and swear to God, hundreds and hundreds of black walnut shells cascaded out of the kitchen ceiling when the water busted through. Some long gone squirrel's Shangri-la. Sheetrock and shells filling the sink, covering the floor. A hundred years ago used to be a farm house for the hands who worked the farm our houses pasture in. Twenty years ago she said she found a Mason jar full of human teeth stashed in a small cavity of the stone foundation down the basement. Once they called, asked me to check the kitchen like they had mouse radar down there in Connecticut and I went over that night following my flashlight beam to the back door. One of them creatures stared eye to eye with me from the dry goods shelf, between the Kraft Macaroni and Cheese and the Campbell's Tomato Soup. Yup. Mice. Aggressive, too. They're good neighbors. Bring up the grandkids to ski the mountains in the winter, and shoot cornstalks and colors with iPhones in the fall for memories.

Pet

My wife elbows me awake.
Clawing and chawing up in the ceiling
has stirred us out of slumber again.
In the quiet dark
the critter sounds more immense
than a mouse—
maybe it's a fisher cat,
or a raccoon.

The gnawing and clawing and chawing
panics us, flat, prone, staring into the universe of darkness—
frozen in fear
over aware of the thin fabric of our PJs,
(we whisper because we are afraid it will hear us),
we imagine the animal will bust through the ceiling
in a shower of sheet rock and splintered wood,
land confused and angry right on top of us
attacking with shredding claws and sharp teeth
when we are at our most vulnerable.

Silently, I recall stories of enraged country folk
peppering their ceiling with buckshot....

The noise unnerves the wife.
The clawing and chewing and chawing halts momentarily,
then commences with renewed vigor.
I say, no way to get at it,
I can't set a trap up there,
or figure out how the beast
got up in the joists on the sloping east side of the roof.

I'm scratching the blueprints in my head
trying to figure out *how the hell…?!*
I helped hammer together this second floor
and there's no way up there—
there's no attic to speak of, just piles of thick pink fiberglass.

Drowsing in the dark, after all of this deep thought,
another elbow spikes me to consciousness,
so I say,
let's call it Pet instead of pest, or
critter, or nuisance, or little bastard,
after all,
think about all we tolerate from family members,
and before she states the obvious, I add,

yes, it's true, none of them lives with us,
but we manage to sleep soundly at night, accepting
their clawing and chawing and chewing
up in the attics of our brains.

Pet will be full and tired soon enough,
he'll quiet down like the drunk relatives
who finally talk themselves out
at weddings, and funerals, and reunions,
tiring of their own tribulations,
realize it's time to go—

the time between those functions
is our layer of insulation between us.

Fire

On successive autumn nights
I burned left-over lumber
from a large summer renovation—
plywood, doors, 2 x 4s—nails and all—
a blaze in a corner of the backyard—
flames leaping ten, twelve feet into the air,
crackling the darkness,
illuminating my face
and my hands feeding the fire.

Weaving in and out
of the sphere of light-licked lawn
on dewy blades
that will be frosted by dawn,

my ten-year-old daughter
danced a pagan dance
like she knew
the light in the darkness
and the warmth of the orange glow
were jubilant discoveries
of things she needed to know.

Invisible Shells

Oddities clutter the studio: a cow skull, worn out shoes, half-baked clay
    pots,
recyclable egg cartons—clear plastic shells cradling pools of paint for art
    students whose
day-dreaming travels well beyond a still life. The warm fall day
inspires the art of escape from invisible shells.
Not even the veteran art teacher can focus, open windows inviting
autumn's sweetness in on bands of dusty sunlight that
revive the longing for
youthful daring and flouting consequences.

School Teacher

And now it's November and darkness
comes early—by 4:30 it's beyond twilight—
do we get more sleep,
our bodies shutting down early,
or do we drink more—or both?
We've already had snow,
sunshine erasing it from yards with little effort,
but more snow today tonight and tomorrow
may stay, cold air from the pole
pushing in on the heels of the storm.
The mud porch is stacked with cord wood.
The atlas on the coffee table
is open to Michigan
and I've been looking at images
of Sleeping Bear Dunes National Shore,
tracing the landscape of the Upper Peninsula
thinking of Nick Adams fishing
the lovely solitude of healing,
examining the roads I'll take
all winter long
in my mind
and wake up to June and a new summer
of long days, my bare feet on that sand,
my eyes sweeping the horizon
of that vast body of fresh water.

The Same Rain

Hunched over in the hard
January rain,
drops ringing in my coffee cup,
the snow melting—
I couldn't help thinking of you.

Was it your leaking roof,
those red Hills Brothers coffee cans
on counters and floors catching
winter rain in your house
and the fog and melting snow
that made you feel invisible
as you looked out your kitchen window
into the cotton white,

then the crushing grind of an airplane
overhead that brought you back?

For a Taste of Honey

Smashed capillaries, ruptured vessels
pooling blood under skin
a tattoo
in the shape of a moth
with blue iron wings—
nothing lace about it, dancing for light—
this one shambles into the darkness
of a long sleeve.

The Dementia Patients

The howlers ceased to moan
the louder the storm raged outside—
they became curious about the larger suffering
outside their heads, listening
to the wind ripping at the trees.

Jealousy Coat

The color of her
jealousy coat,
snappy tailored tight,

is not seaweed green, but
hot baboon ass red.

A garment as old as man—
woven chips of shattered skulls,
fists and shouts,
silence and shame.

The Poison Tree

So soon after the spring of marriage,
he's cooled
by the early frost of love's
birth scars,
so soon after the summer's son.

His frustration is photosynthesized
by the heat of his own passion,
watered by the reign of desire
for uncomplicated tight-bellied dealings.

Swelling, fallen from the poison tree,
the dormant seed
germinates in our skin's earth
waiting there since
an ancient fish breathed on land.

Baptism

At the Christian rock concert
electric guitars throbbed
upside down

when they baptized me in a mud puddle
then tipped me back to where the sky was above again
and all that water slithered like a brown snake
down my face, under my shirt,
between my new breasts,

and then that dirty water crept
right down
where the wet made me shudder.

Secret. Lovers.

Curve of rib.
A cage
she says.

Collar bones,
breasts, sharp,
sudden, amplified
as in a painting.
Waists cool,
piercings tug
meeting moment.
A fingernail
traces
a roadwork of white
razor blade
highways on
taut teenage
bicep and forearm.

Much less
painful
than love
she breathes
between lips
and air.

Alarm

The crow's hoarse caw,
aggressive, threatening,
too close to the open window,
echoed in the gray morning mist,
and then another unseen,
followed by their conversation
of throaty rattles
and indecipherable clicks.

These are the thieves that murder
and devour the defenseless
naked hatched chicks
from other birds' nests.

My discomfort isn't
their robbing and killing,
or that they are fattened
by the flattened carrion
of some unlucky opossum or skunk,
pecked off the road
with veinless beaks,

but their leisure in the indistinct
half-light of the morning,
their raw-voiced prophesies,
their confidence in what is to come.

Drowning in Vermont

When water soaks into the bones
of the dead,
so deep through seams
in all those ancient coffins,
in forgotten weathered marble graveyards
along country roads,

when the water table rises,
and seeps through cracks in concrete,
cellars pooling sorely
against their will,

this spring's drenching rains
is an old argument
that comes back in waves
long after drenched words
have puddled on the floor.

Looking outside at the rain
I think of you
drowning yourself
slowly on whiskey benders
over the weeks and years,
washed out on Sunday afternoons.

Another front of pounding rain
woke us at 4 a.m.
Slowly, saturated with sleep,
we closed windows
against the windblown.
Ebbing my way back to sleep
I could still hear the overwhelming
racket of the deluge
on the roof so close to our heads,
ricocheting off the cars in the driveway,
pelting the ground;

tossing, I dreamt
of you
standing soaked
offering a downpour tumbler
of rainwater to me
in the darkness before dawn.

Recovery

Which one of me is recovering
this morning?
This one's black coffee and ibuprofen.
Red wine tattooed teeth,
garlic slick
dull skull,
peeling back permanent words
like scabs—
the one swearing off drink again—
(it's getting light out,
there's a doe up in the meadow,
and it looks like a clear cloudless morning).

Transfer Station

The man who bullied heaps of refuse
into open-topped freight containers
with a beat-up yellow bucket loader

and signaled to pick-up trucks
to move off the scale
from the door of his heated hut
with caked hands

and collected cash payment
from those who came
to dump their garbage,

recognized the wordless man in the khaki pants
and blue work shirt who materialized
every Saturday morning to comb
the stinking heaps of derelict furniture,
burnt out appliances, rotting food, festering diapers,
broken-spined books, molding Life magazines,
and misshapen bodies of greenblack plastic trash bags,

who sometimes panicked off with a treasure
in his arms as if it were something valuable
that he never meant to discard,
or a shadow he gently clutched to his chest
as if it were a life he could revive,

and didn't mind as long as he stayed out of his way,
even chuckled with others at the possibility of accidentally
scooping him up and depositing the old wacko
into a giant bin with the other trash.

After Mowing

Rain is falling now
on the bloody snake
sliced in slithering unseen—
its body bounced like a baseball
under the mower's deck
and then it was done.

With the toe of my work boot
I kick it
to the ditch.
Once startling design, liquid in motion,
even for a common garter snake, now
a listless rope in higher grass,
food for the sun, flies, and crows.

Looking at it there in the weeds
I felt the trapped panic squeeze my heart,
heard the whirring revolution of the mower,
I felt the sting of blade:
I'll admit it, I don't love snakes
but I know injustice when I feel it.

For the Sparrows in the Newark Liberty International Airport

There's plenty of glass—
windows and weather,
daylight, night,
and seasons to see—

outside, the runways—
planes take off into the stormy
or sunny sky, land with rolling thuds
all day, all night.

How long can a bird survive in a terminal?

I wonder what they eat—
wonder if they're okay with it,
being inside, watching the real world through windows
like a strange movie.

How much I must project
of my life on you, small brown bird.
That's not a glove someone dropped
hurrying to make a connection.
It's a dead bird beneath
the Departures board.

Public Pool

Loud shouts,
shorts down,
pubic hair
stubble shave,
shiny scar,
flab roll,
bursting blue bikini.
Muscle man,
kiddy pool,
naked baby,
diaper waddle,
sun screen,
sun burn,
leather goddess,
season pass,
Marco Polo,
lifeguard
shrill whistle,
high dive,
show boat,
double flip,
belly flop,
French fries,
nachos,
scorching day,
cooling off.

Wild in the Dawn

insane warm windy waking
surging late summer leaves
the maples outside
sound like rushing water
your ears rocks on the river bed

and even 5:30 dim
the sky is a ruddy face
so you stay in bed
while she's raving
half-conscious

feel it brushing your bare shoulder
the curtains panting
to tell you storms are coming
but not loud enough
to completely wake you

after all their words might not be alarm
but dream sleeping keeping
a light blanket on
the hair on your head stirring
slightly like fingers

and I say to her
without words
as I roll over in her direction
if we didn't have screens
our long curtains
would reach out the windows
flashing wild arms in the dawn

Late August

is the lifeguard's swimsuit straps
off her shoulders,
the thin white blazes of skin
hovering over collar bone, daring breast,
descending to shoulder blade;

it's the empty white plastic chairs and chaise lounges,
the few families swimming today,
the reclining man in the white ball cap reading Time;

it's autumn's coolness lurking in the breeze,
and the ripples on the water in the deep end—
enough to remind you of Gatsby,
the green light at dock's end,
gun shot and sinking,
the perpetrator dead nearby;

it's that glimpse of someone
beyond the chain link fence
who has the familiar shape and stride
of a former lover
walking away on green grass
passed the swings and the shiny steel slide
toward the winking cars in the parking lot.

You Were a Blue Lake
In Memory of David Strain

You were a blue lake
edged with dense green forest to the water's edge
reflecting the seasons' sun and weather

until milfoil vines rooted deep,
grew thick and flowered to the surface,
invasive and insistent—

rooted deep, grew thick and blossomed
upwards, invasive, invisible, and insistent.

In the hospital as you slept some restless
cancer-morphine sleep
I expected to see a vine creep
out of your mouth, ripple your surface
with your ragged breathing.

And while that green underwater forest
was taking over, the nature of you was slowing,
schools of your ideas finning in the darkness,
running out of room, running out of oxygen.
Occasionally your hands would take on some task
and I imagined
you were reading book titles
or counting hay bales or coaching some team.

The blue heron of your consciousness waited in the shallows,
and finally with a leap
ascended, defying gravity, spreading enormous wings
to go find you somewhere else.

The Silver Bowl
In Memory of Brian Gawlik

There are four inches of snow
on the green hedge outside of your window
that look as perfect as a birthday cake,
behind it
a leafless winter crabapple
holding white line branches.

It's the first legitimate snow—
inevitable in December.

We've been waiting
for the onslaught of real winter:
blueblack morning's cold house
the somber afternoons melding too quickly into night,
the silencing snow.
And somehow, we're relieved
that it has finally begun in earnest.

I know that you've been waiting, too,
carrying that secret inevitability in your blood,
the same way Nature promises the return of a season.
And somehow, you must be relieved that it has finally begun—
if only to know that it will end,
the dreadful anticipation over at last.

When you were ready to leave us,
I dreamed that I handed you a silver bowl,
large enough to carry the new infant of yourself into spring.

Rob Hunter was born in Syracuse, New York in 1964 and grew up in Attleboro, Massachusetts. He graduated from Hartwick College in 1986, and then from Middlebury College's Bread Loaf School of English with his MA in English. At Bread Loaf he won the Bread Loaf Poetry Prize in 1994. Hunter's first collection of poems, *September Swim*, was published by Spoon River Poetry Press. He was a guest editor of the anthology *Birchsong*, Poetry Centered in Vermont. Over the years his poems have appeared in a variety of print and online magazines including: *Poet Lore, Blueline, Sheila-Na-Gig Online, Oakwood, Rat's Ass Review,* and *Sleet.* He has taught high school English since 1991.

www.ingramcontent.com/pod-product-compliance
Lightning Source LLC
Chambersburg PA
CBHW022128090426
42743CB00008B/1048